Preparatory
Mid-Elementary

A DOZEN A DAY
SONGBOOK

ISBN 978-1-4234-7559-0

WILLIS MUSIC

EXCLUSIVELY DISTRIBUTED BY

HAL•LEONARD®
7777 W. BLUEMOUND RD. P.O. BOX 13819
MILWAUKEE, WISCONSIN 53213

Visit Hal Leonard Online at
www.halleonard.com

NOTE TO TEACHERS

This collection of Broadway, movie and pop hits can be used on its own or as supplementary material to the iconic *A Dozen A Day* technique series by Edna Mae Burnam. The pieces have been arranged to progress gradually, applying concepts and patterns from Burnam's technical exercises whenever possible. Teacher accompaniments and suggested guidelines for use with the original series are also provided.

These arrangements are excellent supplements for any method and may also be used for sight-reading practice for more advanced students.

CONTENTS

Heart and Soul
from the Paramount Short Subject A SONG IS BORN

Use with A Dozen A Day Preparatory Book,
after Group I (page 9).

Words by Frank Loesser
Music by Hoagy Carmichael
Arranged by Carolyn Miller

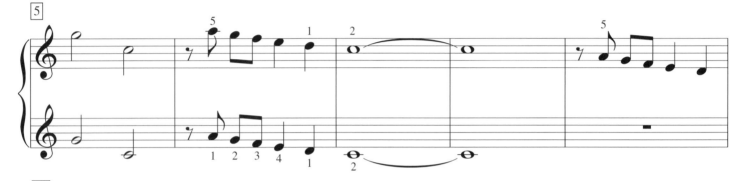

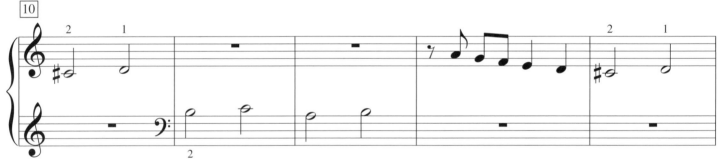

Accompaniment (Student plays one octave higher than written.)

Little April Shower
from Walt Disney's BAMBI
Use after Group I (page 9).

Words by Larry Morey
Music by Frank Churchill
Arranged by Carolyn Miller

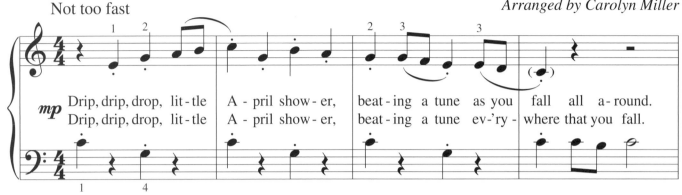

Drip, drip, drop, lit-tle A-pril show-er, beat-ing a tune as you fall all a-round.
Drip, drip, drop, lit-tle A-pril show-er, beat-ing a tune ev'ry-where that you fall.

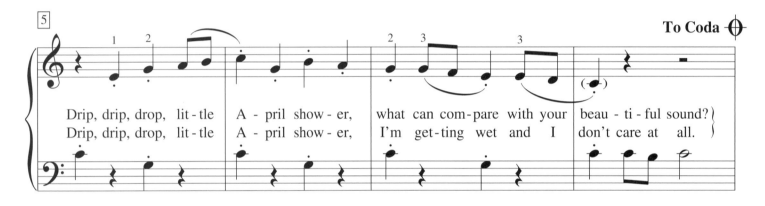

Drip, drip, drop, lit-tle A-pril show-er, what can com-pare with your beau-ti-ful sound?
Drip, drip, drop, lit-tle A-pril show-er, I'm get-ting wet and I don't care at all.

Drip, drip, drop, when the sky is cloud-y your pret-ty mu-sic can bright-en the day.

Accompaniment (Student plays one octave higher than written.)

Drip, drip, drop, when the sun says, "How - dy," you say "good-bye" right a - way.

CODA

Drip! Drop! Drip! Drop! I'll nev-er be a - fraid of a

p   *f*

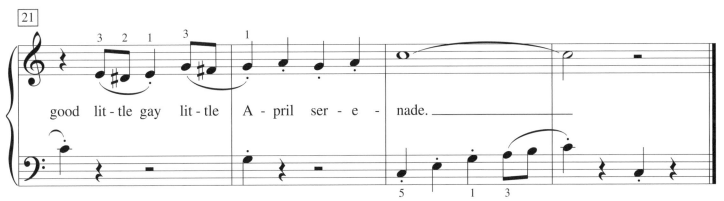

good lit-tle gay lit-tle A - pril ser-e - nade. _____

* **D.C. al Coda** means return to the beginning of the piece, play to the **To Coda** indication, then skip to the measure marked **CODA** to finish the piece.

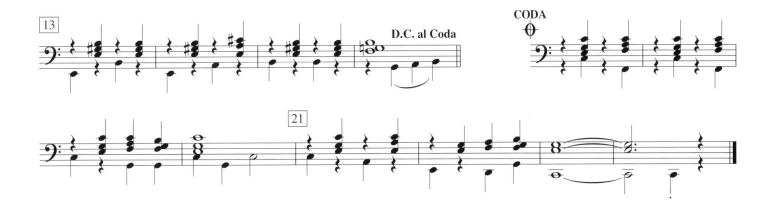

The Way You Look Tonight

from SWING TIME

Use after Group II (page 13).

Words by Dorothy Fields
Music by Jerome Kern
Arranged by Carolyn Miller

At a relaxed tempo

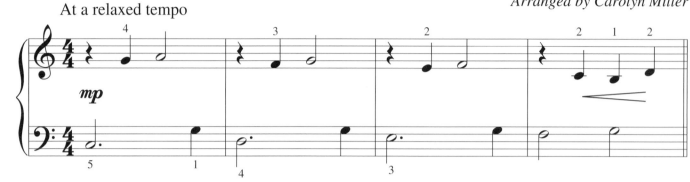

Some - day, when I'm aw - f'ly low, when the world is
love - ly with your smile so warm, and your cheek so

cold, I will feel a glow just think - ing of
soft, there is noth - ing for me but to love

Accompaniment (Student plays one octave higher than written.)

At a relaxed tempo

you
you
and the way you look to - night.
just the way you look to - night.

Oh, but you're

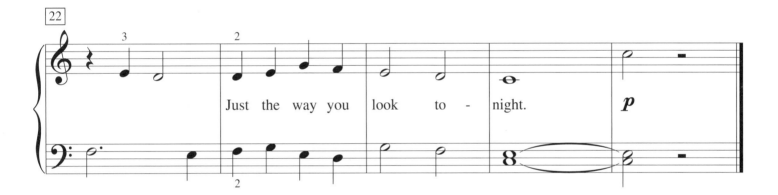

Just the way you look to - night.

p

pp

8vb

Yellow Submarine

Use after Group II (page 13).

Words and Music by John Lennon
and Paul McCartney
Arranged by Carolyn Miller

In the town ____ where I was born lived a man ____ who sailed the

sea. And he told ____ us of his life in the land ____ of sub-ma-

rines. So we sailed ____ up to the sun 'til we found ____ the sea of green. And we

Accompaniment (Student plays one octave higher than written.)

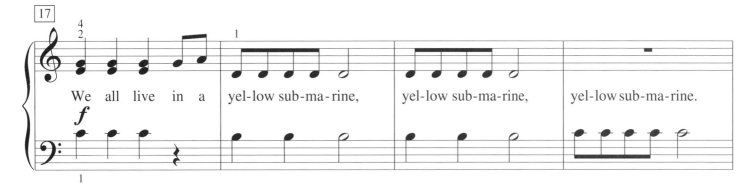

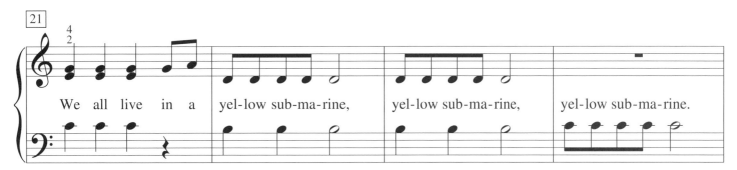

Part of Your World
from Walt Disney's THE LITTLE MERMAID

Use after Group III (page 18).

Music by Alan Menken
Lyrics by Howard Ashman
Arranged by Carolyn Miller

Accompaniment (Student plays one octave higher than written.)

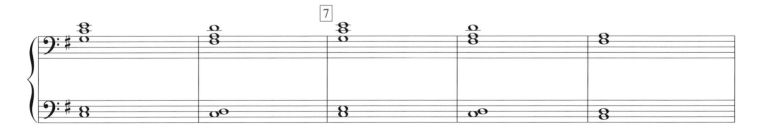

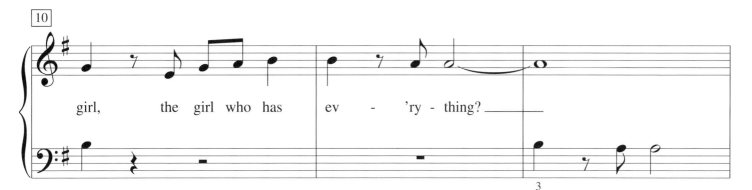

girl, the girl who has ev - 'ry - thing? _____

Look at this trove, _ treas-ures un - told. _ How man - y won - ders can

one cav - ern hold? Look-ing a - round _ here you'd think, "Sure, she's got

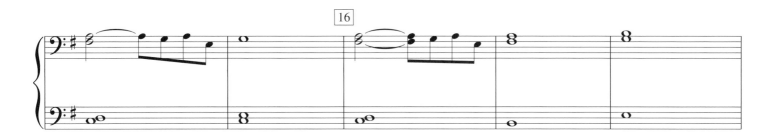

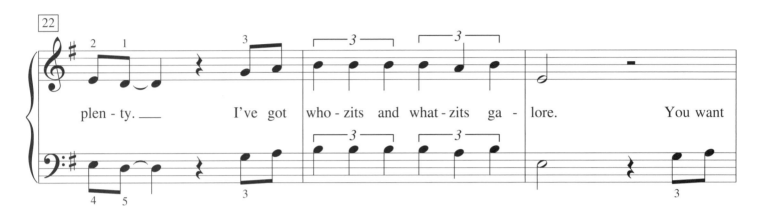

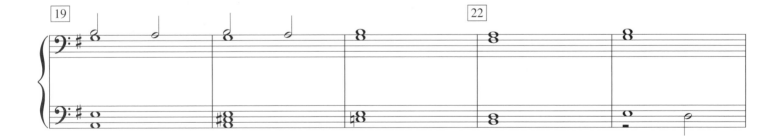

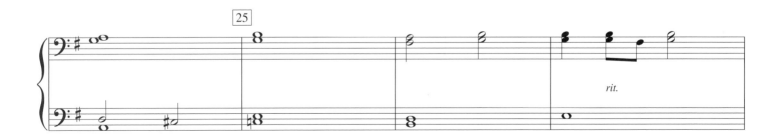

Getting to Know You

from THE KING AND I

Use after Group III (page 18).

Lyrics by Oscar Hammerstein II
Music by Richard Rodgers
Arranged by Carolyn Miller

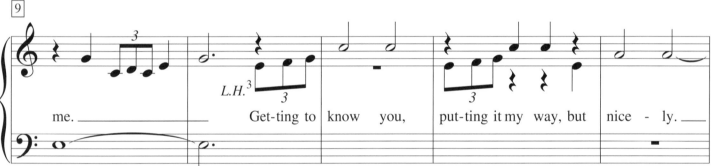

Accompaniment (Student plays one octave higher than written.)

You are pre - cise - ly _____ my cup of tea! _____ Get-ting to

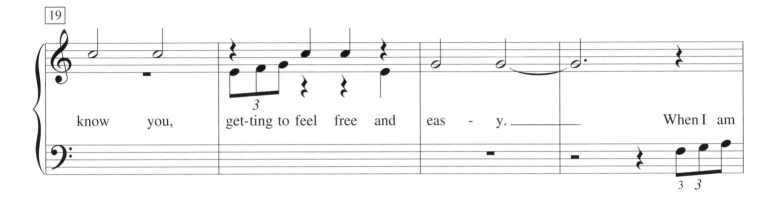

know you, get-ting to feel free and eas - y. _____ When I am

with you, get-ting to know what to say. _____ Have-n't you

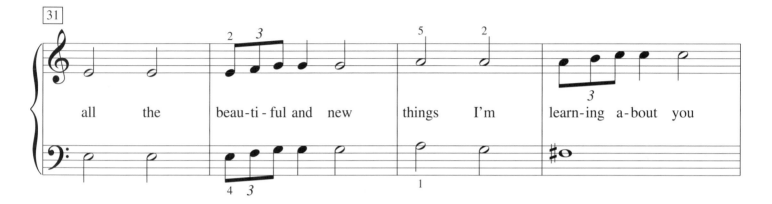

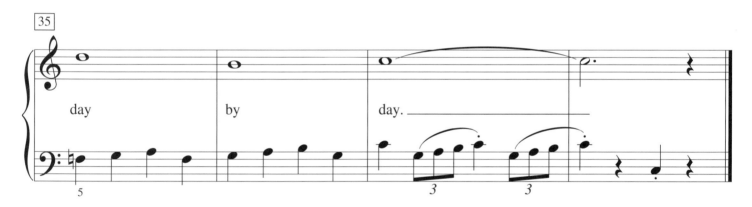

The Surrey with the Fringe on Top

from OKLAHOMA!

Use after Group IV (page 24).

Lyrics by Oscar Hammerstein II
Music by Richard Rodgers
Arranged by Carolyn Miller

Accompaniment (Student plays one octave higher than written.)

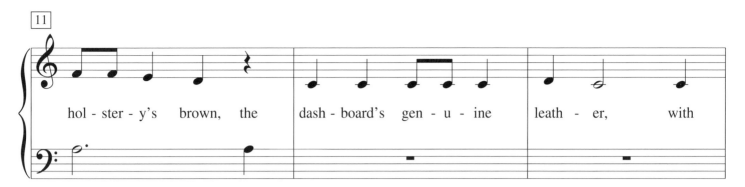

hol - ster - y's brown, the dash - board's gen - u - ine leath - er, with

is - in - glass cur - tains y' can roll right down, in case there's a change in the

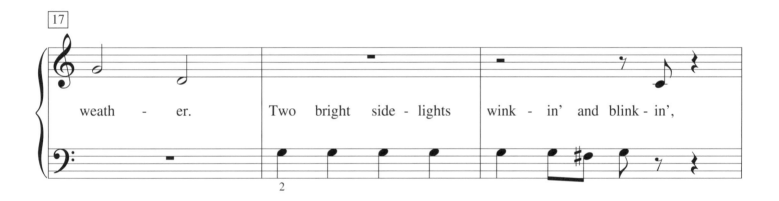

weath - er. Two bright side - lights wink - in' and blink - in',

ain't no fin - er rig, I'm a think - in', you c'n keep your

rig if you're think - in' 'at I'd keer to swap fer that

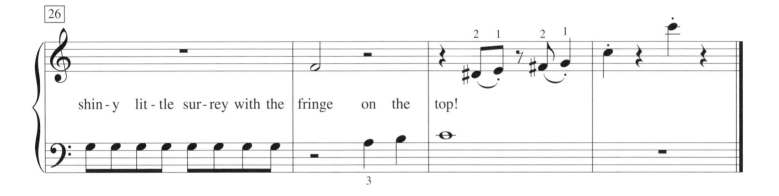

shin - y lit - tle sur - rey with the fringe on the top!

Swinging on a Star

Use after Group IV (page 24).

Words by Johnny Burke
Music by Jimmy Van Heusen

Accompaniment (Student plays one octave higher than written.)

can't write his name or read a book. To fool the peo - ple is his

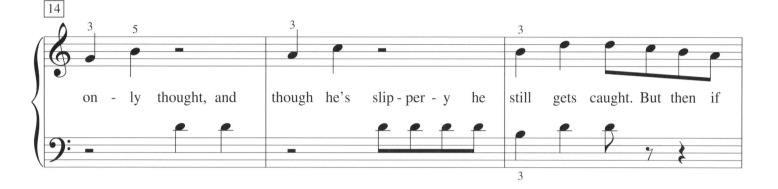

on - ly thought, and though he's slip - per - y he still gets caught. But then if

that sort of life is what you wish, you may grow up to be a

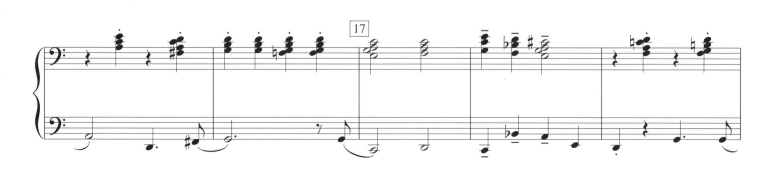

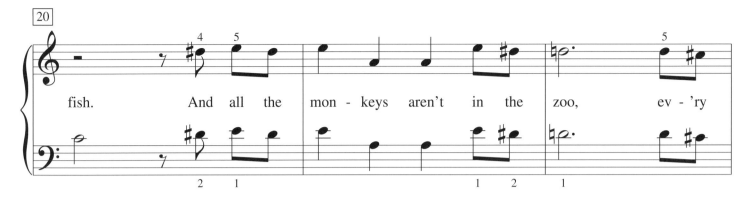

fish.　And all the　mon - keys aren't　in the　zoo,　ev - 'ry

day　you　meet　quite a　few.　So you　see,　it's　all　up　to　you.

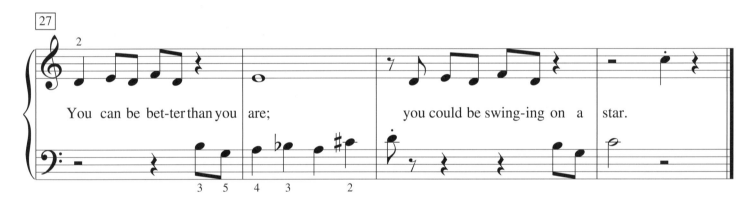

You can be bet-ter than you　are;　you could be swing-ing on　a　star.

The Bare Necessities
from Walt Disney's THE JUNGLE BOOK

Use after Group V (page 31).

Words and Music by
Terry Gilkyson
Arranged by Carolyn Miller

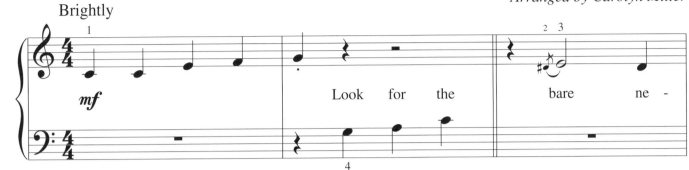

Accompaniment (Student plays one octave higher than written.)

ces - si - ties, oh, Moth - er Na - ture's rec - i - pes that bring the bare ne -

ces - si - ties of life. When - ev - er I wan - der,

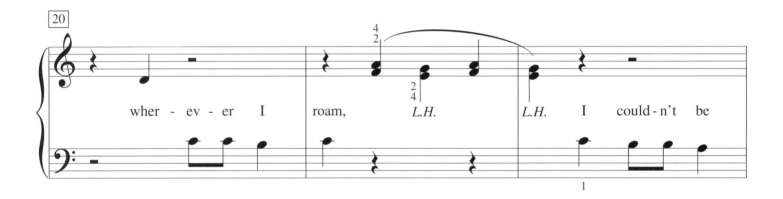

wher - ev - er I roam, *L.H.* *L.H.* I could - n't be

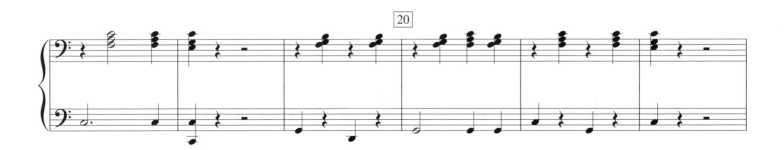

fond - er   of my big   home.   The bees are

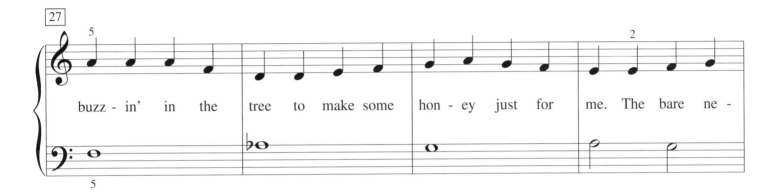

buzz - in' in the   tree to make some   hon - ey just for   me. The bare ne -

ces - si - ties   of   life will come to   you.   L.H.   L.H.

Do-Re-Mi
from THE SOUND OF MUSIC

Use after Group V (page 31).

Lyrics by Oscar Hammerstein II
Music by Richard Rodgers
Arranged by Carolyn Miller

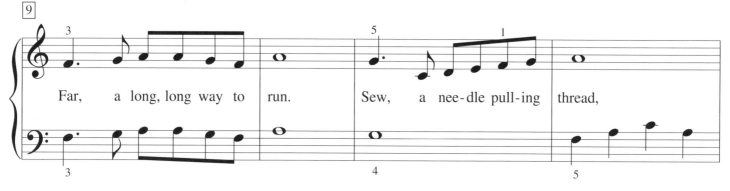

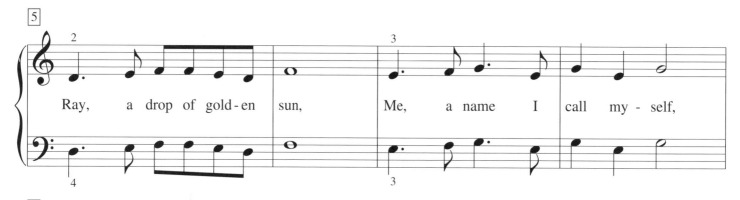

Accompaniment (Student plays one octave higher than written.)

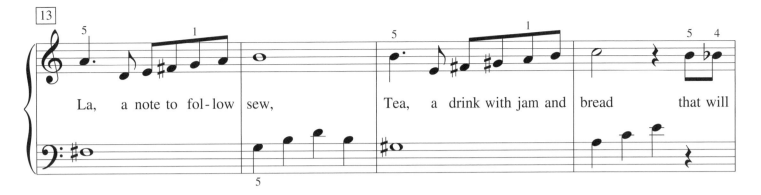

La, a note to fol-low sew, Tea, a drink with jam and bread that will

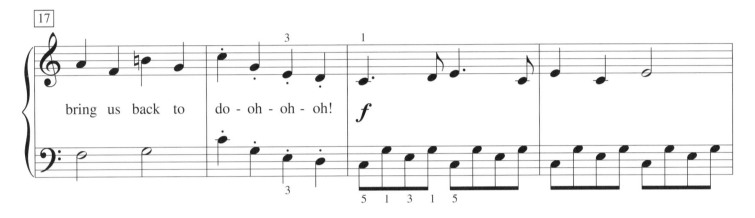

bring us back to do - oh - oh - oh! *f*

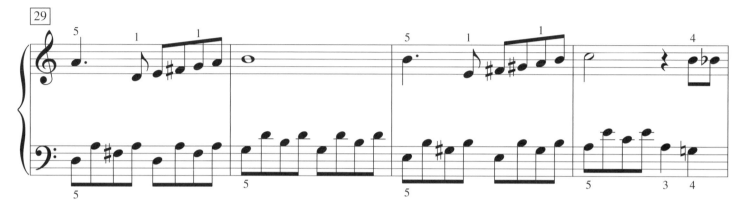

Do, re, mi, fa, sol, la, ti, do! *cresc.* *f*